THE ESKIMO

THE ESKIMO

Arctic Hunters and Trappers

By SONIA BLEEKER

Illustrated by PATRICIA BOODELL

WILLIAM MORROW AND COMPANY
New York, 1959

Grateful recognition is given to Dr. Edmund Carpenter, Department of Anthropology, University of Toronto, Toronto, Ontario, Canada, for reading and criticizing the manuscript.

15   16   17   18

Library of Congress Catalog Card No. 59-5054

Contents

An Eskimo Song

Ai-ai-ai!
I think over again my small adventures
When with the wind I drifted in my kayak
And thought I was in danger;
My fears—
Those small ones that seemed so big—
For all the vital things
I had to get and to reach.
And yet there is only one great thing,
The only thing:
To live to see the great day that dawns
And the light that fills the world.

Reproduced by the permission
of the Department of Northern
Affairs and National Resources,
Ottawa, Canada

I

ON TOP OF THE WORLD

Despite their severe arctic surroundings, the Eskimo are convinced that theirs is the best country on earth. They believe that the spirits were especially good to them to give them such a beautiful land, full of ice and snow, with a coast line chopped up by bays and seas. They believe that the whales, walruses, seals, and fishes that abound

9

in their waters and the musk oxen, caribou, and arctic hares that wander over their lands are special gifts from these generous spirits. These creatures were put there, they say, so that the Eskimo might have ample food and clothing. Through the centuries these strong and brave people have developed ways of making the most of their rigorous surroundings and have learned to live comfortably and happily.

The land of the Eskimo is the arctic region, a central basin filled by the Arctic Ocean and surrounded by land. The Arctic Ocean is, therefore, a landlocked body of water measuring about five and a half million square miles—about one sixth the size of the Atlantic Ocean. Because there is little evaporation in the Arctic Ocean due to its low temperature, and because several large rivers flow into it, its waters spill over into the Atlantic and the Pacific. Most of these waters flow into the Greenland Current. A weaker current, the Labrador Current, comes down through Smith Sound and Baffin Bay, carrying dangerous icebergs that enter the north Atlantic shipping lanes. The water which misses the large outlets into the Atlantic turns westward in a circular movement, bringing warmer waters into the Arctic Ocean.

Except for the ice around the North Pole, which never melts, and the large Greenland ice-cap, the arctic region does not have the vast accumulations of ice that the antarctic has. Most of the land is tundra (tun'-dra), a level or slightly wavy treeless plain. The winters are long and very cold, with temperatures as low as twenty-five below zero. The summers are short and dry. As the sun shines and the air warms in the summer, the surface ice melts, the earth becomes spongy, and plants begin to grow. At this time of year the drab, flat tundra becomes very colorful. The summer is not long enough to permit trees to develop, but there are shrubs, mosses, lichens, and—in early summer—an abundance of brilliant flowers. The banks of streams and rivers, covered with willows and scrub birches, turn a rich green. There is enough vegetable food for the caribou, the musk oxen, the arctic hares, and the reindeer that have been brought in by the governments of the United States and Canada. Birds and fowl flock in by the thousands to breed in these isolated regions.

The Eskimo can be divided into five large geographic groups: the Labradorians, the Greenlanders, the Central Eskimo, the Mackenzie tribes, and the Alaskan Eskimo. In appearance, however, the Eskimo are one people. They are of medium height and thickset, with broad faces, high cheekbones, and narrow eyes. Their heads seem to be exceptionally high and almost pointed. Their skin is really a tawny color, but with exposure to wind and cold their faces get ruddy. Some Eskimo have especially red faces, and the Eskimo say that these people have been cursed by dwarfs.

According to Eskimo beliefs, the dwarfs come down to earth from the sky. Although they are very tiny, they can do everything an Eskimo can do. But no dwarf has the strength to move any-thing an Eskimo has touched. Once, in ancient times, two dwarfs caught a whale and dragged it ashore. But they could move it no farther, and they decided to go for help. An old Eskimo woman and her grandson were standing by the shore, and the dwarfs warned them not to touch the whale in their absence. But when the dwarfs departed, the old woman, feeling hungry, rushed up to the whale and sliced off a chunk of blub-ber. Of course, when the dwarfs returned with several helpers, they could not move the whale, because the Eskimo had touched it. They were very angry with the old woman, and they pointed their fingers at her; whereupon her face began to swell and turn red. Ever since then there have been many Eskimo men and women with very broad and red faces—the curse of the dwarfs.

In addition to their similarity of appearance, all Eskimo speak the same language. It has fewer consonants than ours, and it may sound hollow and gutteral to us. Although the language varies from one region to another, all Eskimo understand each other.

All Eskimo called themselves "the people," or Innuit (in'-u-it). The name Eskimo is comparatively recent. Some people believe that it was given to the Innuit in the seventeenth century by the French missionaries. Others believe that the name Eskimo means eaters of raw meat and was given to them by Indians.

Each Eskimo group also has a local name. Among the Alaskan Eskimo groups are such names as Aglemiut, Chugachigmiut, Kevalingamiut, Nunatogmiut, Tikeramiut, and Ugalakmiut. The ending *iut* means inhabitant of. So Aglemiut means inhabitant of Agle, an Eskimo place name. In Baffin Land and Labrador there are groups like Itivimiut, Sikosuilarmiut, and Tahagmiut. In all, there are about sixty such group names among the Eskimo.

In the nineteenth century, when the Eskimo population was first estimated, there were less than 30,000 people. At present there are about

50,000. The largest Eskimo population is found in Greenland, although the people there are no longer full-blooded Eskimo. In a land where game is constantly getting scarcer, this increase in the Eskimo population has brought pressing food problems.

We know that the Eskimo have been living in the arctic regions for a few thousand years and that, perhaps for a few thousand years before, other people lived in these regions. So far as we know they were skilled hunters, stone-house builders, and ivory carvers, as they are today.

Less than fifty years ago archeologists began to dig for remains in the arctic. The archeologists found many village sites and dug up remains that enabled them to identify and name a few pre-Eskimo civilizations or cultures. The archeologists first uncovered five village sites on St. Lawrence Island, west of Alaska. Since this island is located 150 miles to the south of Bering Strait, the archeologists called the ancients who lived in these villages Old Bering Sea Eskimo. There was no doubt that they were Eskimo, for the remains that were found indicated that their way of life was very similar to that of present-day Eskimo. Their houses were of driftwood, and the chinks were filled with turf and sod, as are the houses of modern Alaskan Eskimo. They used oil lamps for warmth and cooking, and they made clay pottery and carved trays, bowls, spoons, and ivory figures. The archeologists found remains of harpoons, kayaks, umiaks, sleds, and dogs. The Old Bering Sea Eskimo also used ice scrapers and snow goggles. These goggles were made of narrow pieces of wood or ivory that fitted above their high cheekbones and under their brows. Narrow slits permitted the wearer to see but prevented painful snow blindness by reducing the sun's glare. The Eskimo today still make and wear the same kind of goggles.

Digging in the east on the continent of North America, archeologists found more sites. They named the ancient people who had once inhab-

ited this region the Beothuks. Scientists believe
that the Beothuks lived in Newfoundland till the
coming of the first Europeans in the fifteenth
century and subsequent visits by European fishermen and whalers. They still don't know how the
Beothuks died out.

Another discovery of ancient remains was
made around northern Hudson Bay. Archeologists named this the Dorset culture, after Cape
Dorset.

On the flat barrens of central Canada another
culture was found. These people were named
the Thule people. The remains of their homes
were piles of stones, chinked with moss. These
ancients were caribou hunters, whose ways the
Eskimo of central Canada follow today. The
Thulians traveled to the water and harpooned
whales, seals, and walruses in winter. In summer they moved inland to hunt caribou, just as
the Central Eskimo do today. Remains of kayaks, umiaks, sleds, and dogs were found, too.

The remains of another people, the Birniks,

ARCTIC
MELVILL
POINT BARROW
BEAUFORT SEA
MACKENZIE BAY
VICTORI
ISLAN
BERING STRAIT
SEWARD PEN.
ALASKA
NOME
BERING SEA
YUKON R.
FAIRBANKS
YUKON
MACKENZIE R.
MACKENZIE
ANCHORAGE
GREAT SLAVE LAKE
PRIBILOF ISLANDS
CANADA
KODIAK ISLAND
BRITISH COLUMBIA
ALEUTIAN ISLANDS
ALBERTA
SASKAT CHEWAN
FRASER R.
PACIFIC OCEAN
UNITED STAT

were found at Point Barrow, Alaska. They built meat caches of piles of stones and buried their dead in piles of earth. During the summer thaws the archeologists found pieces of carved ivory, yellowed with age.

Moving westward from Greenland, archeologists noted that the islands and peninsulas of the Arctic Archipelago were all settled by Eskimo. But the population was more concentrated in the east than in the west. Greenland and Labrador, the St. Lawrence and Hudson Bay shores, boasted a higher population than the western areas. They also noted that the civilization of the ancients was on a much higher level in the east than it was in the west. Since the culture of present-day Eskimo is similar to this higher civilization, the archeologists concluded that these people must have migrated westward. The Eskimo we know today, unlike the American Indians, came from the *east*, not from the west.

This discovery has changed our thinking about the Eskimo. We believed at one time that the ancestors of the Eskimo came to this continent from Siberia, via Bering Strait, as did the Indians. The Indians migrated from Asia across Bering Strait some 15,000 to 25,000 years ago. We used to believe that the Eskimo had not chosen their frozen home on top of the world, but were pushed northward by the more warlike Indian groups. We now know that these suppositions are incorrect. The ancient hunters of the far north stopped and settled along the arctic shores and learned to live in the arctic as hunters and fishermen. Gradually, over many centuries, a people emerged whom we call Eskimo.

Altogether, the Thule people, the Old Bering Sea people, the Birniks, and the Dorsets were by no means primitive, as were the atlatl or spear throwers who came across Bering Strait 15,000 or 25,000 years ago. These peoples of the arctic were already highly skilled and civilized. We must, therefore, find *their* ancestors to complete the story of the Eskimo's origin. Archeologists today are continuing to study these migrations.

2

THE IGLOO

The Eskimo are nomads. They live in small settlements and move in small units. A group of hunters, with their wives and children, usually spend the winter in one place, however, and we call this place their winter village. But even these winter homes are far from permanent. Sometimes a family decides to visit friends they met at a ceremonial gathering or dance or while they were hunting. This family may leave their original group for a year or two, sometimes permanently, depending on how much game is available in the new area.

On their travels, every member of the family watches the trail, the landmarks, the distances; so all Eskimo, from early childhood, know the geography of their region. Being natural draftsmen, they can readily draw a map of a recent journey in the snow or on a piece of paper. They measure distances in sleeps. At the end of each day's journey the family spends the night in an igloo. This is marked on the map as one sleep. An Eskimo will say that a forthcoming journey may take five or six sleeps, meaning five or six days.

The Eskimo have been called a friendly, hospitable people. They are especially so because they know what it means to a traveler to find shelter and warmth at a day's end. A family welcomes anyone in need and will share food and shelter with him. Often this shelter is already quite crowded, but no igloo has ever proved too small to accommodate another hunter or two.

Understandably, travelers prefer the comfort, warmth, and companionship of an inhabited igloo, no matter how crowded. But if there are no settlements along the trail, hunters can build one in an hour. These hastily built igloos are never very warm or completely dry, but anything is better than facing the cold and wind unprotected. The Eskimo know this and do not mind the effort it takes to build a small igloo, even if it is only for a few hours' rest.

It has been said that the igloo is the Eskimo's most important and most ingenious invention. In a land where there are almost no other building materials, it is indeed an accomplishment to make the ice and snow work for you. Certainly the igloo has enabled the Eskimo to survive his harsh environment.

An igloo in which a man expects to spend his winter months takes many hours to build, for it must be done carefully. The ideal way to build an igloo is for two men to work together. One cuts the snow; the other acts as the bricklayer and lays the snow blocks. For both men experience is necessary to make the kind of perfect structure that can withstand the blizzards outside the igloo and the heat inside. When there is no male helper, the wife lends a hand. Although women lack the strength necessary to handle or cut the huge snow blocks, they have built igloos for themselves when male help was unavailable.

After looking around for a suitable site for their home, a family chooses a snowbank from which to cut the blocks. The man tests it to make sure that the snow did not fall during a strong wind, because such snow falls unevenly and blocks cut from it will crack. Also, the snow has to be just right—not too new and not too old.

Having tested the snowbank, the man and his helper cut into it with snow knives. The snow knife, incidentally, accompanies an Eskimo everywhere he goes. It is made of skillfully joined pieces of driftwood and whalebone or of metal. Because there are no trees in the arctic, the Eskimo have learned to utilize the driftwood they pick up on beaches. They value wood greatly and take excellent care of their wooden tools. With the knife the man cuts snow blocks about three to four feet long, two feet wide, and six to eight inches thick. In some parts of the arctic, the Eskimo use wood saws to cut snow blocks, but the knife-using Eskimo always laugh at these newfangled tools.

After they have cut enough blocks for the base of the igloo, one man begins to lay them in a circle on the ground, while his partner continues cutting. The builder remains inside this circle during the entire operation. His wife and children, in the meantime, may be unloading the sled, getting the dogs unharnessed and tied, or just moving about, inspecting the neighborhood and keeping warm.

The men's capable mittened hands cut and place the snow blocks with ease and skill. The two men banter as they work, thinking nothing of the effort it is taking. Eskimo men and women are used to hard work. It is part of their way of life.

Some igloos are rounded; some are square. If the man is building a rounded igloo, he lays the blocks in a spiral. Each block straddles two of the blocks beneath it and tilts inward, for the Eskimo builder knows that the greater the slant,

the better the support. The upper rows are smaller than the ones below. Thus the igloo has a domed effect, and each block fits closely into the walls with practically no chinks.

The last few blocks have to be handed to the builder through an opening made in the three lowest rows of blocks. With his arms extended overhead, he fits the last few blocks into the ceiling of the perfectly rounded structure. The igloo now measures about fifteen feet in diameter.

Outside the igloo, the Eskimo's wife pats snow into the small cracks between the blocks with her curved snow knife while he continues working inside. He skillfully levels off an elevated area around the walls of the igloo as a sleeping and sitting platform. Then he clears out a few feet of snow from the floor of the igloo so that it will be easier to move about.

There is only a small opening in the igloo to let in the cold air, and the builder begins to feel quite warm. He removes his mittens and loosens the string of his parka, as he continues shoveling the extra snow through the low entrance. It is not good to perspire in this cold climate, for his clothing will get soaked with perspiration, then freeze on his body as soon as he stops working.

After he digs the snow from the floor of his igloo, the man ties up his parka, crawls out, and strides over to where his neighbor has already picked out a snowbank. The division of work is now reversed; the builder of the first igloo cuts the snow blocks, and his neighbor puts them in place.

While this work is going on, the first family moves all its possessions into the finished igloo. The winter day is short, and the woman and children hasten to make the igloo livable. Over the entrance to the igloo, part of a snow block is cut out, and the woman puts a clear piece of sealskin in the opening. This is the igloo's only window. The family tries to keep this window clear, so they can have better light and can look outside. Sometimes a piece of thin, clear ice is placed in this opening.

The large skin cover that is used as the family's tent in summer is hung up under the ceiling and down the walls to the sleeping platform. To hold the cover in place, small holes are drilled in some of the snow blocks, and leather thongs, attached to the cover, are passed through and fastened outside with bone or wooden crosspieces. There is a space between the tent cover and the igloo ceiling and walls that acts as an insulator. The smoke hole in the tent cover is left open, so some of the warm air can escape and some of the cold air can come down. This keeps the air in the igloo circulating.

By the time the cover has been hung, the man of the house has returned to help finish up. He lays the tent poles along the sleeping platform and on top of them piles the sleeping robes and all the furs the family owns. The poles keep the furs from touching the snow and getting wet, and the skins make the platform soft and comfortable for sleeping.

With the igloo finished, the children climb up on the sleeping platform and begin to play. Their mother unwraps the oil lamp, which serves as light, cookstove, and heater for the Eskimo. Soon after it is lit, the igloo becomes warm and comfortable.

Every day the housewife shakes the tent cover so the icicles that have dripped from the igloo ceiling onto the cover will break up and fall toward the bottom of the walls, where they act as extra insulation. After a storm or a snowfall, she and the children inspect the outside of the igloo and patch up any chinks or cracks in the snow blocks with snow. They also scrape and shovel away any snowdrifts that might prove too heavy for the igloo walls. But even with these frequent clearings, snow does pile up around the igloo as the winter progresses, and by the middle of the long winter the igloo may be more than halfway underground.

The tent flap serves as a door for the igloo. Often the low entrance to the igloo is open, but it is protected by a long corridor. This corridor is added to the igloo later, when the builder has time, and very often a second corridor is added at an angle to the first for extra protection against the cold. A corridor is built of snow blocks too. It is long and narrow and about three to four feet high at its entrance. A man can easily walk through the entrance, but he has to bend down as the corridor reaches the living quarters, for its height decreases.

Storage rooms, too, are added to the igloo later. The storage rooms are low, domed structures, also made of snow blocks. From the outside an igloo, its corridors, and its storage rooms look like several igloos of different sizes standing close together.

There is only one way to get to the storage rooms, and that is through the main room, although sometimes they are connected with a corridor. The husband and wife stack their supplies of frozen fish, seal meat, and blubber in the storage rooms. When it is time for the woman to prepare a meal, or when a child feels hungry, she crawls into the storage room and chops off a chunk of frozen fish or blubber. The Eskimo have no fear of anyone's stealing their food. A stranger, if he is hungry, will help himself. What they are afraid of is that their ever-hungry dogs might get to the food cache. That is why the storage rooms are connected with the main room—to keep the food safe from the dogs.

The dogs remain pegged close to the igloo. The cold does not bother them, for they are well protected with heavy coats of fur. They bury themselves deep in the snow and curl up, so that only a dark tip of a nose sticks out. The Eskimo dogs are only partly domesticated, and they have been trained to obey no one but their master. It is never safe for a stranger to approach an igloo too closely without calling out to those inside. The owner must tell his dogs to lie down before the stranger can come near.

Late in 1957, the U.S. Army's Greenland Research Program came up with a plan for housing that utilizes the principle of the igloo. The engineers were anxious to save fuel costs, which are enormous in that region. Three quarters of the cargo that leaves the United States for Greenland is fuel.

With a tremendous plow, called a Peters Plow, the engineers dug a trench twenty feet under the ice and put up twenty-four huts, resembling igloos. It is hoped that the U.S. scientists will spend comfortable, warm winters in them from now on, protected from the storms and blizzards that rage over the Greenland icecap. Igloolike warehouses can also be built there, to store planes, trucks, and supplies.

There are several other kinds of winter homes in different parts of the arctic. Where there is ample lumber or driftwood, homes are made of logs. In western Alaska, for example, the igloo is definitely only a temporary shelter, put up by a hunter or by a family traveling to visit rela-

tives. The western Alaska Eskimo builds his
house partly underground, both for warmth and
for sturdiness. These semisubterranean houses
are made of stone, earth, and driftwood logs.
The men and women dig into the ground as far
as possible; this is only a few feet, however, because the ground is always frozen farther down.
They line the floor and walls with stone and
earth and build up the roof and the upper parts
of the walls with driftwood logs. The logs are

chinked with moss, and the roof is covered with earth for warmth. They always leave an opening in the roof for the smoke hole. These houses are usually one-room dwellings, even though more than one family may live in them. A wide platform made of logs is built either in the back of the room or along three walls. There the family or families sleep and the children play in the evenings or in very cold weather.

In winter the entrance to the house is closed, and a low, semisubterranean corridor is built. This corridor is also covered with earth, and people crawl through it into the main living room.

In other parts of the arctic, homes are built like the rounded Indian tepees. Being short of wood in these areas, the Eskimo make the frame of the house out of whalebone and cover it with sod. If walrus hide is available, the women sew several hides together and use them as a tent cover. In order to keep out the cold and yet have some light, the Eskimo housewife puts a piece of ice into the roof opening. But as the air in the house warms, it rises up and melts the ice. The ice drips on the floor, making it soggy, muddy, and slippery. So these "tepees" are not as comfortable or as warm as the igloo or the subterranean house.

For those who know how to take care of themselves amidst the ice and cold, the arctic can be friendly and enjoyable. And so the Eskimo, who have learned how to build houses that keep them warm and dry, can live comfortably in their frozen world.

3

INSIDE THE IGLOO

The Eskimo lamp, a necessity for survival in the arctic, is, like the igloo and the semisubterranean house, thousands of years old. The lamp matches the igloo in its simplicity, ingenuity, and usefulness. It, too, makes use of native materials: stone, blubber, and moss. Most lamps are made of soapstone, which is found in many parts of the arctic. Because it is soft, soapstone can be carved quite easily. All Eskimo are excellent carvers in wood and ivory, which are much harder materials than soapstone, so the making of a lamp presents little difficulty once the stone has been obtained.

The lamp itself is a flat, shallow, oval-shaped dish with two compartments. The fuel for the lamp is blubber, which comes from seals, walruses, and whales. It is the coat of fat next to their skin. Blubber for the lamp is at its best after it has been frozen, for the oil it contains will come out naturally in the unfreezing process. During the short summer, when blubber does not freeze, it is much harder to get the oil out. Then women and children chew the blubber and spit the oil into a small dish. In the winter the housewife places the frozen blubber right into the smaller compartment of the lamp. As the blubber melts, the oil from it flows into the larger compartment. There the housewife puts a fringe of twisted dried moss or sedge, which she has picked from the tundra during the summer, then dried and put away for winter use. The moss is ignited, and it acts as a wick, sucking up the oil and burning with a steady flame.

As long as the lamp is burning, the housewife tends it with a piece of bone or wood. She straightens the wick as it burns and presses it into the oil if she wants a larger flame. Because of this skillful care, the lamp does not smoke. A

lamp is never left unattended. When the housewife has to go out, her daughter or, occasionally,
her husband, tends it. But as a rule this is the
housewife's job, and the lamp is always placed in
the corner of the platform where she sits.

Over the lamp the Eskimo housewife balances
a square-shaped frame for drying clothes and
boots. The frame is made of wood and is sup-
ported on four poles. At the top of the frame
are two horizontal poles and from them hang
two kettles. One kettle is for stew; the other is
used for melting snow.

All drinking water in the arctic is melted snow
or ice. Every morning a boy or girl goes out
with a hatchet and brings in a lump of snow.
The Eskimo housewife drops it into the kettle,
and whenever anyone in the household is thirsty,
he can ladle himself some water. Sometimes the
ice that has formed out of sea water is melted
and used for drinking. Old ice is used, for curi-
ously enough, it does not have a salty flavor, although it comes from salt water. Only freshly

formed ice has a salty flavor. Ice that is several
years old is as pleasant, when melted, as fresh
water. The salt seems to evaporate after a long
period of freezing. The Eskimo, incidentally,
have always disliked salt and still do today. No
matter how hungry they are, they will not eat
salted food. But they have learned to relish sugar
and sweets, although there were no sweets in the
arctic in the old days.

Eskimo meals are usually simple, and there is
little variety in the daily food the housewife pre-
pares. Their most important foods are meat,
blubber, and frozen fish. In this cold climate,
fat is as essential as meat, and when blubber is
not available, people develop a craving for it.
The contents of the stomach of a freshly killed
seal or walrus are also relished.

In the evening the family forms a circle
around the hot kettle of stew. The father scoops
up a chunk of blubber or meat with his hand.
He bites into the chunk and with his knife cuts
off a slice close to his lips. He passes the chunk

on to his wife, who also bites into it and cuts off a piece. Then she passes the remainder to the children.

When the kettle is empty, the mother fills each person's cup with tea. The Eskimo let the tea cool before drinking it, for they dislike hot food. Both tea and coffee, as well as tobacco and sweets, were introduced by the European and American traders, and the Eskimo took to them very quickly. On their trips to the trading post they regularly select packages of tea, coffee, sugar, and tobacco in exchange for their fox pelts and bearskins. The Eskimo housewife uses her tea and coffee sparingly, for since they come from so far away, they are quite expensive. Tea leaves and coffee grounds are cooked over and over again till they have no flavor or color left.

Before the introduction of tea and coffee, the Eskimo drank quantities of water after meals and occasionally brewed herbs for medicinal purposes. But today tea has become as much a part of the Eskimo diet as blubber. Even on the trail a family will stop every few hours, not only to rest the dogs but to warm themselves by drinking a few cups of tea. Often this drink is the only food they have until evening.

When the teakettle is drained, the meal is finished, and dishes and cups are cleared away quickly. They are wiped clean with a piece of fur or moss and set in back of the lamp for the next meal. Father lights his tobacco pipe and stretches out on the sleeping platform. Mother also lights her pipe. Eskimo women enjoy smoking, and often, when a child cries, a mother takes her pipe out of her mouth and gives it to the baby as a pacifier.

The Eskimo love to eat, but overeating is not considered good manners, except at a feast. To teach their children moderation, parents tell them a story about a boy who ate too much. One day the boy went hunting. He caught a seal and ate all of it. Then he speared a salmon and ate it, too. He next harpooned a whale and ate the whale. Having eaten so much, the boy felt thirsty and went to the lake to get a drink. He drank and drank until he had drained the lake.

When he entered his igloo to rest after all this eating, his mother warned him not to get near the oil lamp. The boy obeyed her, but the lamp moved toward him. Suddenly there was a terrible explosion. The boy blew up and was never seen again. In his place were a seal, a whale, and a salmon, floating in the calm lake that had formed in the center of the igloo after the explosion.

In the arctic, the game supply may vary greatly from year to year and season to season. Periods of plenty are all too often followed by periods of scarcity. These are terrifying times. Hunters go out day after day and return empty-handed, till they are too weak to go out or to seek better hunting grounds. Often blizzards force the hunters to stay indoors. During this period the family eats up all the stored food; then they eat the dogs and all the scraps of leather to be found around the house. They even chew again on the cracked bones that litter the floor—discards of meals eaten in happier times. Parents will go hungry for many days so that their children can have the last scraps of food. Finally, when all hope is gone, a mother may kill her children to end their suffering. When food is again available, those who survive quickly regain their strength and move away, leaving the settlement, with its sad memories and buried dead, behind.

It is believed that in these extreme times some

Eskimo used to resort to cannibalism. But these instances must have been very few. No one will ever be sure about this, for most of the information we have is hearsay.

The Eskimo are very hospitable people. A hunter and his family would rather go hungry for the entire winter than hold back any food in the storeroom when guests arrive. When strangers come to an Eskimo settlement, they are usually entertained in the home of the best hunter, since his storeroom is well filled. With great humility, the hunter invites his guests into his "poor home" and offers them some of his "poor food," which he says is unfit for the dogs. Hesitantly, and with many apologies, he crawls into his storeroom and brings out some delicacy he has saved for just such an occasion. This may be a mixture of fat, blood, brains, and bone marrow, which has been put into skin bags and frozen. Or perhaps it is frozen narwhal skin with blubber, which is always eaten raw. The host protests that he will be shamed forever for

offering such bad and spoiled food to such distinguished guests.

By this time, since news travels fast, everyone
in the settlement has already crowded into
the hunter's home. People sit close together, the
men in the front, the women and children in the
back. The host now cuts off a piece of the frozen
narwhal skin with blubber, chews it, and spits it
out on the floor in disgust. "This is the worst
food," he comments. He pretends that he is
about to throw the whole mound to the dogs.
His guests and neighbors begin to protest, insist-
ing that this is just the food they want. The
host relaxes, a broad grin on his face. The hostess also beams with pleasure. Her husband's by-
play has been well received. The guests will
have a wonderful feast.

Each man now takes his turn cutting off a
large chunk of skin and blubber with his own
knife. Then he passes the food behind him to
his waiting wife and children. The guests stuff
themselves and belch audibly to impress upon

the host how much they are enjoying the food. The host and hostess are almost too happy to eat.

Frozen auks are another delicacy which travelers will talk of for a long time. These little sea

birds have thickset bodies and very short wings and tails. To us they look almost like tiny penguins. (There are no penguins in the arctic, of course.) In the summer auks come to the arctic by the thousands to nest and raise their young.

Men, women, and children catch them with a net and collect their eggs. They gorge themselves on the eggs and save the leftovers for storage and later use. The birds are stuffed into a sealskin.

When a host serves such a stuffed sealskin, he is sure that his guests will enjoy every morsel. But custom calls for more apologies. He bites into a bird and spits it out as unfit for human consumption. Again he pretends, as his wife beams over his good manners, that he had better throw it to the dogs. And only the loud protests of his guests force him to put the sealskin down in front of the distinguished assembly.

The host and hostess watch as each guest digs into the sealskin and extracts a bird. Every bit of it is eaten. First they pull the skin back from the bill until it is turned inside out, and eagerly suck the tasty oil in the skin. Next they pull out the feathers and swallow the entire skin. Then they pick the flesh off the bones. Finally they chew and swallow the bones, which are very soft.

Again the guests belch to show their appreciation, and the host and hostess are overcome with pleasure.

Now the hostess is ready with a kettle of boiling tea. The guests wash the fat off their hands and wipe them on a piece of fur, then reach for the steaming cups of tea.

By this time everyone in the house is hot. The guests remove their shirts and lean back contented. Now is the time for entertainment. In every settlement, no matter how small, there is always a man who is considered the best singer. This man is expected to start the entertainment. But, like the host, he has to be coaxed. He will begin by saying that he has lost his voice, that he has forgotten the songs, and that his voice is no good anyhow. But after much coaxing he steps forward. An Eskimo song is very simple. It is a tune with few words. Singers always dance, too. A dance in a crowded igloo is a swaying movement in rhythm with the song. The singer repeats the song many times, his voice rising higher and higher as he sings, "Ai-ai-ai, aa-aa-aiaa!" Usually a singer ends his song with a shriek. This makes the people laugh, and a singer is very happy if people laugh when he finishes his song.

Inspired by the success of the first singer, another man gets up. With a little less coaxing this time, he begins to sing and dance. Sometimes, swayed by the rhythm and the happy mood, even a shy woman will get up and sing in a high-pitched voice. Others follow, until almost every man in the settlement and even some of the strangers have had their turn.

Despite all the noise, many people, especially the children, fall asleep, overcome by their full stomachs and the heat of the room. No one disturbs the sleepers. After a while the neighbors begin to drift back to their homes, leaving the strangers to sleep either on the ledge or on the floor—wherever they can find room.

Since the lamp is allowed to go out during the night, the igloo turns cold. Each person takes his dry boots and stockings, his pants and shirt, and rolls them up in a bundle. He puts the bundle under his head. By doing this he provides himself with a comfortable pillow and at the same time keeps his clothing dry and warm. Asleep in their fur sleeping bags and robes, the Eskimo do not mind the cold. They do mind getting up to a cold igloo, but the housewife always gets up first and starts the lamp going for the rest of the family.

Long after everybody is asleep, the woman sits up mending or sewing a new pair of mittens or stockings for a member of the family. An Eskimo usually owns no more than one complete suit of clothing. Each piece of clothing, however, is tanned, sewed, and mended by the housewife. Eskimo styles in clothing vary from locality to locality, but they all have one thing in common—they are designed to keep the Eskimo warm and dry. Both men's and women's clothes are made of sealskin and fur. They consist of stockings, boots, trousers, a fur shirt, and a roomy jacket or parka of heavy fur that usually hangs to the knees.

The stockings, made of deerskin, fit over the knees and are tied with thongs. Before putting on his boots, with their heavy walrus soles, a man adds a pair of slippers made of bird skin, the feathered side worn next to the foot. The three layers of footwear keep him quite warm.

His trousers are made of fur, doubled over so that there is soft hair against the skin as well as on the outside. These trousers hang below the knees and are tied around his waist with a thong. His parka has a small hood with a drawstring that fits tightly around the face. There are also drawstrings around the sleeves and at the bottom to keep the snow and water out. Winter parkas are trimmed with wolverine fur. This fur sheds snow and water, and the long hairs blow over the wearer's face, protecting him from the sharp winds. To trap or shoot a wolverine takes much skill, and when a family wears clothing trimmed with this fur, it shows that the man is a brave hunter. In the summer, when the ground is wet, a man wears sealskin boots and pulls a loose-fitting sealskin parka over his head.

Eskimo women wear two pairs of trousers. One looks like a pair of shorts and is usually made of the soft fur of a deer's belly. The second pair of trousers fits below the knees.

Strips of long-haired fur are used to decorate women's clothing, and animal teeth are added as ornaments to tassels on trousers and leggings.

Also, the men drill tiny holes in the teeth and string them into necklaces for their wives.

A woman's parka is long-sleeved and roomy, with an enormous hood that reaches to the middle of her back. In this hood she carries her baby as long as it is nursed—until it is about two years old. When the baby is in the hood, the woman ties a belt around her waist to hold the hood in place.

The baby is dressed in fur. Its one-piece suit is made of fawnskin, and a fawnskin cap covers its head. The mother leaves the baby's legs bare, since it is warm enough in the hood. Inside the igloo the baby does not need shoes, for it usually crawls about on the sleeping platform in the warm fur bedding.

Until they are about eight years old, boys and girls wear the same clothing: boots, trousers, and parkas. After that, boys' clothes are the same as the men's, and girls' clothes are like the women's. Most parents feel that they need not dress their daughters in fine clothing once they get older, so they are given the poorest skins. It is to the credit of an Eskimo man that his wife is fat and is dressed in the best furs. When his wife accompanies him on his trading trips, everyone will see that he is an able hunter and a good provider. But a daughter soon marries. It is up to her husband to feed her well and provide her with fine skins for her clothes.

When a caribou is killed, the man always saves the sinews of its back and legs. His wife uses sinew as thread. It is dried and beaten until the fibers loosen and separate. Then the fibers are cleaned. Before she starts sewing, the woman soaks some of these fibers in a little bowl. As the wet sinew in the seam dries, it will shrink and make the seam watertight. In the old days a woman used a small bone awl to make tiny holes in a seam. Then she pulled the sinew through the holes. Today most Eskimo have steel needles, but they still prefer sinew to store thread.

The men value expert sewing. As a rule, Eskimo men and women are modest and shy away from praise. A hunter will never boast to anyone about how many seals he has caught in a season or how many valuable arctic foxes he has trapped. He answers modestly any questions about his hunting. He will say, "I am getting old. I am a poor hunter." Yet a man will praise his wife's sewing and show off the handsome clothing and boots she has made. A man with faulty seams in his boots or with poorly matched furs becomes the laughing stock of his friends. In fact, an Eskimo may even leave his wife because of her careless sewing.

When a man comes home, he shakes the snow off his parka in the corridor of the igloo and leaves it hanging outside. It is better for the fur to be kept at a colder temperature. Wearing only his undershirt and trousers, he steps down into the igloo. Once inside, the warmth of the igloo envelops the tired hunter like a comfortable blanket. Soon he takes his shirt off, too. But first he sits down on the platform, removes his boots, and hands them over to his wife. They get a careful inspection, for if anything is wrong with them the hunter's toes may freeze. She carefully goes over the rough spots. Then, her needle ready, she rubs and fingers the boots to make them pliable and squeezes any water out of them. Finally she inspects the seams. If any need mending, she fixes them before putting the boots on the drying rack of the lamp. Later, after the evening meal, she will also inspect and mend her husband's fur stockings before she puts them on the rack to dry.

When not pressed by immediate needs to dry clothes or cook food, the woman takes out her scraper and begins to scrape a new caribou skin for tanning. It is against Eskimo custom to work on these skins before the first seal is caught. After a caribou hunt, the skins are rolled up and put away until the time is right for scraping and tanning.

After the inside of a skin has been scraped clean, the housewife rubs every inch of it with caribou brains mixed with urine, to make it soft and pliable. Once a skin has gone through this tanning process, it will remain soft, provided that it is dried carefully every time it gets wet. That is why the Eskimo are so careful about drying their boots and clothing.

When visitors and their wives come to an igloo, the women join their hostess near the lamp and go over their husbands' footwear. However, when two hunters traveling alone visit an igloo, they hand their wet boots to the hostess. She puts them into shape again, mending and drying them just as she does her husband's boots. This is part of Eskimo hospitality, another custom that makes life more pleasant in the harsh environment of the arctic.

4

KAYAK, UMIAK, AND SLED

Eskimo depend on wildlife for almost all their needs. Since wildlife does not remain stationary but moves with the seasons, the Eskimo have to move with the seasons too. Their life is full of wanderings and adventures on land and sea. Every day the hunter, with the help of his trusty kayak, sled, and dog team, pits his skill and luck against the elements.

The Eskimo calendar contains thirteen months, and each month has twenty-eight days. The seasons are not evenly divided as ours are. There are six months of winter; the remaining seven are spring, summer, and autumn. Every now and then the Eskimo leave a month out of the year and so manage to keep their months in the right seasons. The new moon marks the beginning of each month, and the old moon marks its end.

Spring and winter are the times for hunting sea mammals—the seal, the walrus, and the whale. Summer and fall are the times for hunting the caribou and for fishing. Polar bears and musk oxen are hunted all year round.

The Eskimo believe that all the animals of the land and sea were created by Sedna, a beautiful girl who lived with her father, Anguta. (Anguta, some Eskimo believe, created the earth, the sea, the sky, and the stars. Other Eskimo groups believe that Raven was the creator.) Whenever a young man asked Anguta for his daughter in marriage, Sedna made her father refuse him. No one was good enough for her. But one day the fulmar, a large arctic sea bird, came to woo her. He promised her a warm, newly built igloo lined with fur, and fine meals of meat and blubber. Beautiful Sedna, for some reason, believed his promises and consented to marry him. But when she followed him to his home she found that it was a dark cave in a cliff, full of fishskins. And instead of meat and blubber she ate only fish and more fish. Sedna soon tired of this life. She waited until her husband went fishing and then cried out to her father to rescue her. Anguta immediately got into his kayak and came to take her home.

However, the neighboring fulmars, seeing Sedna depart, followed the kayak and called upon the high winds to create a storm to drown her and her father. Afraid for his life, Anguta threw Sedna into the water so the storm would abate. But Sedna held on to the sides of the kayak. Anguta then pulled out his knife and slashed off Sedna's fingers at the joints to keep her from holding on. Each joint, as it floated away, turned into seals, walruses, and whales. That was how these sea animals were created.

Sedna sank out of sight, the storm abated, and the fulmars departed. Anguta then called out to his daughter that all was safe. He hauled her into the kayak and took her home. With the aid of his magic her fingers soon healed. But Sedna never forgave her father for his cowardice, and she plotted revenge. One night, when Anguta fell asleep, Sedna called to her dogs and ordered them to chew off her father's arms and legs. Anguta awoke in great pain. But even greater than his pain was his indignation that his daughter should plot revenge. He began to chant a magic song that caused the earth to open and swallow him, Sedna, her dogs, and the igloo. Since then the creators, Anguta and Sedna, have lived underground, watching over the Innuit from below.

It is said that old Eskimo who die natural deaths go to live in the darkness of the underworld with Sedna and Anguta. Those who die violent deaths, either by drowning or by deliberately freezing to death when they grow too old to hunt, go up into the sky worlds. There they live happily ever after in lands of snow and light, filled with sea and land animals, which they can hunt to their hearts' content. Even today, old people are anxious to choose their own manner of dying, so they will be assured of a happy afterworld amid the ample snows overhead.

Although the Eskimo spend most of their life on or near the water, they do not, as a rule, know how to swim. It would be useless for them to learn, for the water is extremely cold. If a man does fall into the water, he quickly freezes to death. Actually, the Eskimo are afraid of the sea, for it takes too many lives each season. In their light kayaks (ki'-acks), however, the Eskimo can go everywhere. A kayak is safe enough in expert hands, and the Eskimo is very sure of himself in his boat. He calls his kayak a man's boat. It does take a man's strength to get the most out of it.

It is a one-man canoe made of driftwood and sealskin, so light that it can be easily carried by a boy. It draws no more water than that much cork. Since archeologists have found kayak frames among the remains of ancient arctic civilizations, the kayak must be several thousand years old. It is certainly an invention of the arctic peoples.

Putting together the framework of a kayak is the man's job, and it requires great skill. An Eskimo fits pieces of driftwood together, ties them with sinew, and hammers them together with wooden pegs. The shape of the kayak differs somewhat among the Eskimo of Alaska, Greenland, and Labrador, but all kayaks have a heavy, round cockpit made to hold a single man. This cockpit is well fastened to the rest of the frame. All of the hunter's gear, as well as his game, gets tied to it.

The sealskins for the kayak are prepared by the woman. First the skins are carefully scraped; then they are stretched and sewed around the framework while wet. When the sealskins dry, they shrink and fit snugly against the frame.

Some Eskimo use a single paddle; some prefer a double paddle. They put two ivory rings on the paddle, so the water will drip off them instead of running up their wrists and sleeves.

The kayak is used all over the Arctic Circle all year round, wherever there is a lane of open water. In this light craft a man is ready to face the roughest seas, and he can even navigate a waterfall. For sport the Eskimo turns somersaults in his kayak and comes up dry, his clothing protected by the sealskin. With much practice a man learns to sit in the kayak all day long, his legs outstretched, without moving. This is much harder than staying in a saddle all day. When tired, he pulls his drawstring hood about his face and slumps forward in the kayak for a nap. He makes sure that all his gear—his sealskin floats, his precious harpoon, and his paddle—are secured to the kayak, for sometimes sudden storms come up. In such an emergency a hunter guides his kayak onto an ice floe and rests there till the storm blows over.

The umiak (oo´-me-ack) or, as the Eskimo call it, the woman's boat, is really the family boat. It is roomy enough to hold a family, all their household goods, and even a friend or two. This boat is wide and flat-bottomed, with seats and high sides. It is not built for speed or grace, and it has neither of these qualities. It is just a com-

fortable and safe boat in which nomad families can travel from one place to another.

To make the framework of an umiak the men lash wood and whalebone together. After the framework is finished, the women lash on a walrus-skin cover. The cover is so large that it fits over the gunwales. It is tied to the inside—over the thwarts and the framework—with long thongs. When not in use, the umiak is dismantled. The framework is lashed to a high platform, and the walrus cover is folded and put away for future use.

In the umiak women paddle and a man steers. Often a man accompanies his family in a kayak, hunting in his boat and guiding the umiak over rapids or through rough seas.

The distances the Eskimo have to travel on land are best covered by a sled drawn by a team of Huskies. The sled is another ingenious device made of native materials: driftwood, leather thongs, bone, antlers, and ivory. An Eskimo cares for his sled with just as much concern as he does for his dog team, his harpoon, and his boots.

The kayak or umiak can be loaded onto the sled, for it is built to carry heavy burdens over rough ice and snow. A sled may be fifteen feet long and up to two and a half feet wide. It has two runners connected by crossbars. The runners

are wide in front and narrow toward the back. This construction distributes the sled's weight over a wider surface, making the sled more stable. The runners are curved in front, and some have a special shoeing of whalebone or ivory. Sometimes mud is put on the runners. It is shaped and polished and allowed to freeze. Then water or urine is poured over it and also allowed to freeze quickly. This shoeing is good

for a while. But the ice wears off, and the driver has to stop every few hours to re-ice them once more.

The back of the sled is often made from deer antlers. The points of the antlers are removed, leaving only the stubs. The driver leans on them and controls the sled.

A team is made up of anywhere from six to a dozen dogs and bitches. They are solid, well-knit animals, with large, broad heads and strong chests and backs. Their feet are enormous. The lead dog is the strongest and is feared and obeyed by the rest of the team. Some Eskimo prefer a bitch for the lead, because she seems to make the other dogs obey her. The dogs' harnesses, made of either sealskin or caribou-skin thongs, pass under the forelegs and join over the back and chest. A hole is drilled in the crossbar in the front of the sled, and the dogs' traces are pulled through it. When harnessed, the lead dog has the longest trace. Behind follow two other strong dogs, then the dogs that are less strong. The weakest are tied closest to the sled.

The sled is usually completely loaded and the load tied down with leather thongs before the team is harnessed. Then, should the dogs start running unexpectedly, the sled will not spill. After the dogs are harnessed, the master gets behind the sled and away they go. If the load on the sled is light, the driver may sit down on top of it or let his wife sit down. Usually some members of the party run ahead of the dogs to keep them moving at a fast pace.

A dog team has to be handled carefully and skillfully to get the most out of it. The driver has to watch the road ahead to make sure there are no big bumps that might injure the sled. Sometimes there are large cracks in the ice, and it calls for skillful guidance to get the sled over them in one piece. The driver shouts and clacks his tongue at the dogs, uttering all sorts of bird and animal cries to spur them on. He has to make sure that his whip touches the dog whose name he calls. If he calls to one dog and lets his whip down on another, the two dogs will stop and fight each other. The driver leaves it to the lead dog to straighten out any fights. The lead dog usually snaps at both dogs, and they are subdued. The driver and his companions dare not talk to one another on the trail. If they do, the dogs stop to listen. The driver may also have difficulty when he adds a new dog to the team. The dogs are loyal to their teammates, and when a strange dog is placed among them, they will often refuse to pull the sled. The strange dog, in turn, may chew at his traces, break away, and return to his former home and teammates.

Once the sled gets going, it is very hard to stop it, for the Huskies, although raised in the household, are only partly domesticated. Their wolf ancestry asserts itself all too often. The Eskimo know this. When a driver wants to stop, he must pull the back of the sled and dig his heels into the snow.

Traveling by dog sled is easier in winter than in spring and fall. As the snow melts, thin, jagged edges of ice remain on the ground. A trail of jagged ice can damage the dogs' paws, and the Eskimo often put shoes on them to prevent this. A driver must stop and inspect the shoes every so often to make sure they are not torn or slipping off. At night he must dry them just as he does his own boots. This is a great bother, but it is worth it if all the dogs survive a strenuous trip with little damage to their paws.

The Eskimo hunters value their dogs, even though they often treat them roughly, kicking

them out of the way and whipping them on the
road to get the best out of them. When there is
ample food, a man feeds his dogs once a day;
when there is not, the dogs are fed every other
day. Some Eskimo prefer to feed their dogs in-
dividually. This prevents jealousy and keeps the
stronger dogs from grabbing food from the
weaker ones. When an Eskimo goes hungry, his
dogs go hungry too, getting leaner and more
wolflike. An Eskimo kills a dog for food only
when it is absolutely necessary.

When the Eskimo hunt for seals under the
ice, they travel by sled, going as close to the
water's edge as the ice and snow permit. Seals
prefer freshly formed floes, enormous pancakes
of ice that form in the arctic seas. The seals
scrape breathing holes in them and come up
through these holes to sun themselves and to
sleep. The sight of these dark spots on the horizon—seals that are sunning themselves—is most
welcome to an Eskimo hunter.

When hunting, the Eskimo watch to see what

phase the moon is in. They know that high tides come with each new moon, so at that time they are careful to allow for the incoming high tide when they are camping near water. The high tide may also cover up the breathing holes in the ice, and then the hunters must wait for the tide to recede before they can look for them.

Sometimes, if there are many breathing holes and so the hunters expect to spend much time in one place, they build a blind of snow blocks and arrange their gear behind the blind. If several hunters work together, one of them remains behind to mind the dogs, while the others creep on ahead. They approach the floes cautiously. Above all, the seals must not be frightened, or they will quickly disappear under the ice. The hunters get as close to the seals as safety permits; then they throw their harpoons. The harpoon, thrown like a spear, is a long shank with a triangular, detachable head. The head has a sharp piece of stone or metal in it, and a thong is attached to it. When the head sinks into the animal, the hunter keeps hold of the thong. The wounded seal begins to struggle, and sometimes it jumps into the water. The hunter lets it thrash about until it is exhausted; then he pulls it up.

There are many kinds of seals. The earless seal has been called the mainstay of the Eskimo. Other northern seals—the fur seal, the bearded seal, the ringed or fiord seal, the harp seal, and the hair seal—all feed around the arctic shores and are game for the Eskimo. These seals weigh anywhere from 150 to 800 pounds. No seal is too small or too large for the Eskimo hunters. Sealskins, especially those of the pups, are highly valued. The fur seals gather in rookeries in the spring, and there the adults mate and their young are born. The adults teach the young to swim, and later they leave together for warmer waters. Eskimo hunters reach these rookeries in their kayaks and harpoon all the seals they can carry away.

The Eskimo hunters know the habits of each kind of seal. They avoid the fighting bulls in the rookeries. Instead, they skirt around the rookeries where the bachelor adults stay. The hunters charge into the mass of seals and harpoon them before the seals become aware of the danger and scoot for the water.

The ringed or fiord seal prefers quiet waters. The female digs a long tunnel in the snow, where she has her pup. The Eskimo locate this tunnel, crash through its roof, and harpoon both mother and pup.

The hungry men and dogs can hardly wait for the hunter to cut open the seal's belly. But before even the hungriest man dares to bring the warm food to his mouth, the Eskimo hunters pause to thank Sedna. They also thank the harpooned seal for letting itself be killed. The Eskimo believe that if a hunter forgets to give thanks to Sedna and to the spirit of the seal, he may never catch another seal.

Having thanked Sedna and the seal for their generosity, the hunters cup their hands and quickly drink the warm blood that spurts out of

the seal. Then they eat the partly digested food in the intestines. The seal belongs to the man who harpooned it, and he passes around some of the blubber and chunks of the seal's liver. Eskimo are fond of liver. They eat the livers of all animals as soon as they are killed. But they do not eat the livers of the bearded seal and the polar bear. These livers are poisonous.

Some of the remains of the seal are thrown to the dogs. Then the seal is skinned, and its carcass is rolled into the skin and tied to the sled with thongs. The hunters keep on hunting until their sleds are loaded.

The walrus is distinguished from the seal by its larger size and its ivory tusks. The huge, almost hairless body of the walrus is ten to twelve feet long and may weigh up to three thousand pounds. Both males and females have tusks. The male's tusks droop from each corner of his mouth, and they are sometimes over two feet long and weigh up to nine pounds. The female's tusks are more slender and have a curve in the middle. Both the male and the female use their tusks as shovels for digging on the sea bottom for shrimp, starfish, clams, and other sea life. The male also uses his tusks for fighting. It takes a walrus two years to grow tusks, so the female walrus nurses and cares for her pups during this time. At the end of the two years they are able to get their own food.

The Eskimo want the walrus not only for its tusks, meat, and blubber, but for its heavy hide. Walrus hides are sometimes up to three inches thick, and they make excellent covers for umiaks and tents.

In the old days it was quite a feat to harpoon a walrus, and a hunter was happy to get one or two a season. The walrus rests on the ice for long periods at a time. If an Eskimo is careful not to let a walrus get his scent, he can get quite close to it and throw his harpoon. Nowadays, with the use of guns, walrus hunting has become less difficult and less dangerous. Guns are used for hunting seals, too.

Year after year the Eskimo hunters are on the lookout for whales. A whale carcass will furnish an entire village with meat and blubber for a long time. Going after a whale is a long, co-operative undertaking. It involves all of the village's man power, sleds, dog teams, kayaks, and umiaks. The men make floats of inflated seal-skins and attach them to the thwarts of an umiak. They put extra-heavy twelve-foot shafts on their harpoon heads. When a whale is sighted, the Eskimo man their loaded umiak and, paddling at a steady pace, head for the spot where the whale blew. The man who is to throw the first harpoon stands in the bow, noting the time between the whale's surfacings. He must throw his harpoon the moment the whale surfaces. If he misses, he tries again and again, until the harpoon sinks in. The whale dives below, pulling against the floats, the heavy umiak, and the harpoons. When it surfaces again to get air, the other men in the umiak strike it with their harpoons.

As a famous naturalist once said, "There are whales and whales." Some, such as the blue whale, reach a length of 100 feet. Others, such as the white whale and the killer whale, are only five to fourteen feet long. Some whales have teeth; other whales are toothless and have rows of whalebone that hang from their upper jaws. These are the whales' mouth strainers. As a whale moves, it opens its mouth and water pours into it. With its huge tongue it forces the water out again through its strainers. The small sea life the water holds remains inside the whale's enormous mouth and is swallowed.

Sometimes when a whale is pursuing food, it ends up stranded in shallow water. The whale's skeleton is not made to hold up its weight on land, and the whale flounders for a time in the shallow water, then dies. The Eskimo, always on the lookout for a stranded whale, try to get to it before the wolves, foxes, and polar bears do.

For many centuries the Eskimo were able to

get enough whales without making much of a dent in the yearly supply. In the nineteenth century, however, whalers from all over the world began to invade the arctic waters. Hundreds of whalers set forth from the United States ports alone. The whalers were interested in whalebone and ambergris. Whalebone was used for ladies' clothing, and ambergris, a substance found in the sperm whale's stomach, was used in making perfume. With so much whaling going on, whales became scarce, and today they are no longer a reliable source of food for the Eskimo. Whaling is now restricted to certain seasons, although the Eskimo are permitted to hunt whales at all seasons.

With the coming of Europeans and Americans to the arctic, other wildlife also diminished in numbers. Otter fur was in great demand, and everyone hunted otters, regardless of season, until they were almost exterminated. The seal and the walrus were also killed off mercilessly. The Alaskan fur seal became so scarce that the governments of the United States, Great Britain, Japan, and Russia agreed to control the hunting of seals. The United States is now operating the fur-seal industry. This agreement, made in 1911, was renewed and ratified by the Senate in August of 1957. The yield of sealskins in 1957 was 93,618, the biggest since the agreement came into effect.

With less game to hunt, the Eskimo found themselves in a sad predicament. Many of them could no longer feed and clothe themselves by

hunting and trapping independently. They had to find substitutes for the meat and blubber so essential for survival in the arctic. Fishing helped some, but the people could not live on fish alone. And they also needed skins for their winter clothing.

Efforts to solve the Eskimo's food and clothing problems were begun about a century ago by the governments of the United States and Canada. It was common knowledge that the people of Siberia in the Arctic zone (the Chukchee, for example) had a way of life similar to that of the Eskimo. But about half the Chukchee owned large reindeer herds, which assured them, as it did the Lapps of Europe, of a steady food supply and skins for clothing. With this fact in mind, the governments of the United States and Canada invited herdsmen from Lapland, as well as from Asia, to bring in reindeer and teach the Eskimo how to herd them. Our government began by importing sixteen reindeer in 1892 and continued importing small numbers of them until 1902. By 1928 there were 80,000 reindeer in Alaska. It is estimated that arctic and sub-arctic Alaska can support three to four million head of reindeer. Arctic Canada, experts say, could support thirty to forty million head.

But it takes a long time for a people like the Eskimo, who have been hunters for many centuries, to become herders. Today, in some areas, the reindeer have not been killed off fast enough. Without supervision they have overgrazed their terrain. Nevertheless, the future is promising.

The two governments have also been considering the possibility of teaching the Eskimo to domesticate the musk ox. Musk oxen can be milked, and they would provide Eskimo households with much-needed milk, butter, and fat. This might relieve the Eskimo mother, who often has to nurse a child for two or three years, because there is no other milk available. Also, musk-ox fur supplies excellent wool for clothing.

Some Eskimo now work for the United States Government in Alaska, hunting fur seals. They also work in Alaskan fisheries and fish canneries. With the money they earn they can buy meat and flour and store clothing. It is hoped that someday soon the Eskimo will face a more secure future.

5

INLAND HUNTING

Legends among some Eskimo groups tell that the goddess Sedna had been worrying about the Innuit. She had been listening to their prayers for food, and she knew that her people were starving. There had been storms all over the arctic, and the seals and walruses would not come within reach of the hunters. Sedna, therefore, decided to create land animals.

The first animal Sedna created was the caribou. To her the caribou, with its heavy antlers and flattened face, was very ugly. Its body was stocky, and the fur on its belly and neck was shaggy. Sedna looked at the creature in disgust and decided then and there to run away from it. But the caribou followed her. Although she ran fast, the caribou ran even faster. There seemed to be no way of stopping it. Sedna threw a rock at the caribou to frighten it and knocked out its front teeth. That is why, to this day, the deer family has such poor front teeth. But the caribou continued to follow her. Then Sedna threw a stick at it. The stick sliced off the caribou's tail, which is why the deer family has such stubby tails. Still the caribou followed her. Pleased with its swiftness and persistence, Sedna decided to let the caribou multiply, despite her own dislike of it. The caribou herds grew until they covered Canada and the arctic regions. They became the Eskimo's chief source of meat in the summer.

To this day the Eskimo are very careful not to offend Sedna by eating caribou meat at the same time that they eat the meat of her favorite creature, the seal. They fear that Sedna might be offended by the smell of venison and destroy the caribou. They also believe that a seal will not let itself be harpooned if the blood of the caribou is on their hands when they hunt it. Eskimo women do not even tan deerskins until the first seal has been caught, for fear of offending Sedna.

In the old days the caribou wandered by the millions over the arctic tundra. The eastern half of Canada, including the polar regions, used to be the home of the woodland caribou. The western half of Canada, including the Mackenzie region, and Alaska were the home of the Barren Ground caribou. Today the herds of woodland caribou in Canada have greatly decreased. The Barren Ground caribou are still numerous, although they are being replaced by the semidomesticated reindeer, which are relatives of the caribou. In a way, the caribou are a menace to the reindeer owners. When a reindeer herd meets a herd of caribou, the reindeer tend to mix with the caribou and are lost to their owners.

During the winter herds of caribou wander about in the snow, digging deep holes in it and searching for lichens and mosses, which are their chief foods at this time of the year. On this meager diet the caribou lose their fat, but their

fur is at its best. Their undercoats are a fine
wool, and the long hairs of their outer coats are
shaped liked quills—hollow and filled with air.
Their fur keeps them afloat and warm in the icy
arctic waters. Herds of caribou will cross any
body of water in their path, paddling through it
swiftly with their big strong hoofs. When caribou travel by land, these split hoofs spread as
they walk. This keeps them from sinking into
the snow or into the soft, spongy soil of the
tundra during the thaw.

With the coming of the warmth, the herds
begin moving south. The cows give birth to
their single fawns in May or June, but this does
not slow down the herds. The fawns are able to
follow their mothers soon after birth. The herds
are on the move for two reasons. They want to
escape the swarms of flies, ticks, and mosquitoes
that come with the warm weather and mercilessly attack the defenseless caribou, getting into
their eyes and eyelids, their nostrils and ears, and
under their skins. They also need food. Farther

south there is more young grass and common sedge. Willows and dwarf birches are eaten eagerly after the meager winter diet, and the caribou begin to accumulate fat.

This is the time of year when the Eskimo become tent dwellers and followers of the caribou. The tops of their igloos begin to melt in the warmth, and gradually even the walls begin to shrink. The soil of the arctic never thaws more than six inches, however, even during a warm summer. The subsurface is always frozen. The water from the thaw forms marshes, and traveling by sled becomes impossible. Even with a light load a sled will sink into slush, and the dogs cannot pull it out. So the Eskimo build high platforms on which they store their sleds for the summer; then they load their tents and household goods into umiaks. Guided by the men in the kayaks, the women row the umiaks south, trying to get there ahead of the caribou.

When the Eskimo reach their destination, they spread out, for there is not enough firewood in one place to supply a large group. Families set up their tents on elevated ground, where it is breczier. The household arrangements inside a tent are very much like those of the igloo. Toward the back of the tent is a raised platform, made of brush, over which the family throws its furs and skins. This is the family bed. Also in the back are fur bags containing household goods, and a wooden box or two. Every Eskimo housewife owns such a box. It holds needles, extra belts, thongs, decorations for clothing, and the family amulets. Extra clothing is hung from crosspieces on the ceiling of the tent.

In the front are the living quarters and the kitchen. The living room of the tent, like that of the igloo, soon gets cluttered with leftovers and scraps: pieces of fur from the clothing, fishbones, fish heads, meat bones, and chips of wood. The kitchen is used only when the housewife is driven indoors by rain. Most of the cooking is done outside. The cooking place is a circle of rough stones. Near it is a pile of twigs and brush and any other dry, burnable material the young-sters and women can collect.

When they are not cooking or sewing, the women spend their time gathering berries and sedge. The berries are a delicacy. Those that are not eaten at once are dried for later use. The moss and common sedge are also dried and stacked in small sacks for use in lamps. If a woman expects a baby, she will gather a lot of moss, because dried moss is also used as diapers. The mother puts it into her hood whenever she puts her baby there. She also spreads dried moss on the platform, where the child sleeps and plays, until it is trained.

While the Eskimo are settling in their tents, the caribou are moving south. Day after day the tramping of thousands of hoofs shakes the tun-dra. The clicking together of small ankle bones can be heard long before the caribou are sighted. To the Eskimo hunters, waiting along the trail for the caribou to come, it is a joyful sound.

Any living thing in the path of this mass mi-

gration will be trampled to death. Hunters and
their families always stay on the fringe of the
herd, watching. In the old days, when the Eskimo had only bows and arrows, they hid behind
rocks and hummocks and shot at the nearest caribou, then waited for the herd to pass before
claiming the carcasses. Nowadays, with the use
of guns, it is easier to slaughter caribou in larger
numbers. Unfortunately, there are much fewer
migrating caribou today. Sometimes when a
herd is sighted, the Eskimo hunters erect a stone
barricade along the caribou's path, forcing them
to detour through a narrow gully or swim
through a neck of water. The animals are then
singled out and shot. When a caribou is struck,
either by an arrow or by a bullet, it does not move
immediately. It stands still for a few seconds,
giving the hunter a chance to aim and shoot
again and again until it is dead.

In summer, when the herds break up, the Eskimo work in pairs to hunt single animals. One
man walks closely behind the other, and in their

fur clothing they look as brown as the caribou.
They hold their bows and arrows over their heads
to resemble antlers and imitate the grunts of the
caribou as it grazes. If the grazing animal looks
about suspiciously, the two men lie down and

pretend they are a caribou resting. Sometimes
one of the hunters even wears a caribou's head.

Walking in the summer is always difficult, because the ground is soft. When the Eskimo go
out to hunt caribou, they try to carry as little as

possible, for a heavy load will make their feet sink into the ground. Hunters use a quiver made of sealskin, which holds a large bow, extra bowstrings, extra sinew for repairs, and about a dozen arrows with stone or bone points. The bow is made of horn. The man makes the bow by splitting a horn and splicing the pieces together with wet sinew. The bowstrings, of carefully twisted sinew, are usually made by his wife.

When a caribou has been killed, the hunters thank Sedna for her generosity. They cut up the animal, roll it up in its skin, and carry or drag it home. It will be tanned later, after the first seal has been caught. The family feasts on the animal's insides—heart, liver, and intestines. Some of the meat is cooked for the evening meals, and some is made into pemmican. The meat is cut into thin slices, pounded, mixed with berries and fat, and then dried. It will keep indefinitely. Pemmican is a highly concentrated food, and a small quantity goes a long way. Eskimo hunters like to carry it on trips.

Although the caribou is the Eskimo's most important source of food in the summer, it is not their only source. In the summer, as well as in the winter, the Eskimo hunt the musk ox, the polar bear, and the ptarmigan.

Some people believe that the musk ox is one of the oldest animals of the arctic. It thrives amidst ice and snow and, unlike the caribou, it never migrates, for its heavy coat cannot be penetrated by insect bites. With its broad hoofs it shovels away the snow and feeds on the mosses and lichens underneath. It enjoys the fresh vegetation that the summer brings—grass and horsetails, saxifrages and birches, all sorts of berries, and, especially, young willow shoots.

The musk ox is a shaggy animal, smaller than a buffalo, with an exceptionally long-haired coat. The hair on its back, mane, and belly is sometimes as much as two to three feet long. Its hair is straight, except on its shoulders, where it curls; and it is dark brown to black in color. Unlike the caribou, the musk ox has horns—permanent fixtures. These curve down and then sideways, and they get larger with age. The musk ox is neither slow-moving nor does it have a musky odor, as was claimed by early explorers.

The Eskimo hunt musk oxen with the help of their dogs. When the dogs locate a musk-ox herd, they begin to bark and leap about, keeping the animals at bay until the hunters arrive. By this time the bulls in the herd have arranged themselves in a circle, as buffaloes do. The cows and calves remain inside the circle, and the bulls face the attackers.

A wounded bull is dangerous. Enraged and in pain, it will attack dog and hunter. It is a swift runner, for its hoofs have horseshoelike ridges on them which grip the ground. The Eskimo hunters often lose their best dogs on musk-ox hunts, and if a hunter is not quick enough to dodge a charging, maddened bull, he will be gored to death.

A while back, when the Eskimo began using guns, musk-ox hunting became easier. In fact, so many musk oxen were slaughtered that the governments of the United States and Canada had to restrict musk-ox hunting even for the Eskimo until there was no longer any danger of their becoming extinct.

All year round the Eskimo hunters keep a sharp lookout for a chance to get a polar bear and its valued white skin. Polar bears do not migrate either. They hunt and fish in the arctic waters the year round. Only the pregnant females hibernate. They remain in a snowbank from early winter to March. There they give birth to a pair of pups and suckle them through the winter months. The best time to hunt polar bears is in early October. The skins and the tender meat of the young are highly prized.

The ever-present ptarmigan (tar'-mi-gan) often rescues an Eskimo family from starvation. Many times, when a hunter returns home empty-handed, he finds the stewpot full, because his son has shot a ptarmigan or two. This large bird is white in winter, when it wanders inland along watercourses. Its gray summer plumage camouflages it, blending with the gray of the lichens and mosses on which the ptarmigan feeds as it moves north. The meat of a ptarmigan is sufficient to feed an entire family, and its feathers are most welcome as a lining for boots and for bedding.

In the spring and summer the arctic is a haven for all sorts of birds. Migrating fowl—ducks, geese, and gulls—come by the thousands to breed in the cold waters. Innumerable varieties of smaller birds—sea, shore, and land birds—come to nest. Terns and thrushes, swans and swallows, sandpipers, scoters, sparrows, magpies, and mallards descend upon the arctic, their varied colors making the landscape glow.

Eskimo boys raid the birds' nests and eat their fill of eggs. Since the domesticated chicken is still unknown to most of them, this egg harvest is a treat for the Eskimo family. The young raiders, however, are aware that they would destroy a good part of next year's birds if they took all the eggs out of the nests, so they always leave some for hatching.

All Eskimo boys and girls, from the time they are eight, help to get food in the spring, summer, and fall. A boy has a simple bow, made of wood or horn, and arrows of willow twigs or polished pieces of driftwood, with blunt, rounded heads. During the long summer days, when it seems as if the sun will never set, boys wander about with their bows and arrows, snooping, climbing, and looking for wildlife. They learn the habits of all the birds and animals and become excellent imitators of their calls. This knowledge is invaluable to the hunter. When Eskimo are hungry, no animals are too small for the cooking pot, and the boy who brings them in begins to be regarded by his family as a hunter. However, to be accepted among the adult hunters, he has to harpoon a seal or shoot a bear or caribou. Often a father helps his son accomplish this. He lets the dogs hold a bear at bay and maneuver it so that the boy is the first to spear or shoot it. Everyone then congratulates the boy on his achievement. Later, the bear meat and fat are used for a feast to celebrate the boy's entering manhood.

The fox and the otter are also important to the Eskimo, since their pelts are used for clothing and for trading. As soon as a boy reaches his teens, he is given traps and is expected to care for them in all kinds of weather. The Eskimo try to visit their traps daily. It is important to kill an animal as soon as it is caught, for a struggling fox can damage its fur so that it is worthless at the trading post. Bad weather often keeps a trapper from his daily inspection, especially nowadays, when game is scarce and traps are set miles apart. But it is not unusual for a boy to walk five to ten miles a day in sub-zero temperatures. Girls and young married women also set out traps and walk great distances to tend them.

In the past the Eskimo did not value fox and otter pelts any more than they valued other pelts. Trapping foxes and otters was always considered boys' and women's work. The early traders, to whom the fox and otter pelts were most valuable, could not understand why the Eskimo hunters refused to do trapping. They thought the men were lazy. But after the traders got to know the Eskimo better and saw the tremendous effort they put into their daily hunting, they realized that they were wrong. The hunters were not lazy; they refused to tend traps because they were ashamed to be doing women's or boys' work, even though the pelts could be traded readily for the guns and ammunition that they needed. After a while, the men turned to trapping, but it was quite a struggle for them to overcome an ancient custom.

For the Eskimo the hunting of animals is a never-ending activity. Whether they are harpooning seals in the winter or following the trail of the caribou in the summer, they are always in search of food and clothing.

6

ESKIMO CUSTOMS

The activities of the Eskimo are determined by the seasons and, of course, by the weather. During the dark stormy months of winter, when the sun hardly shows itself above the arctic horizon before it disappears again, hunters are confined to their homes for days at a time. In the summer, during the weeks when the sun does not set at all, the Eskimo lose all sense of time, and hunters often paddle about in their canoes until they are exhausted. People are up at all hours, and there is always noise and laughter outside. Visitors barge in at all hours, too, expecting to be fed and entertained. This constant activity exhausts even the sturdiest and hardiest Eskimo. Many of them confess that although they look forward to the sun and warmth during the severe

winter, they feel relieved when the weather begins to turn colder, the sun begins to set, and
their lives resume a regular day-and-night
routine.

Some Eskimo settlements have a large community house, where people gather together and
cook food, feast, dance, sing, and play games.
This house is used in summer and in winter.
Where there is no community house, people visit
one another to help pass the time. When the Eskimo men are not involved in getting food for
their families, they catch up on their sleep, clean
their guns, mend their hunting and fishing gear,
carve the walrus tusks they have set aside, play
games with their children or with their neighbors, and tell stories.

Eskimo men are gifted bone, stone, and wood
carvers. When a man harpoons a walrus and gets
its ivory tusks, he does not immediately decide
what he will carve out of them. Instead, he takes
the tusks to the igloo and lets them lie there for
a while. Whenever he has the chance, he han-

dles each tusk, examining its shape and its im-
perfections and weighing it in his hand to get
the feel of it. Gradually an idea forms in his
mind as to what he should carve from this piece
of ivory. By the time he brings out his files and
drills for carving, he knows just what the finished figure will look like. With this image in
mind, the Eskimo say, it is very simple to make
a good carving.

The Eskimo carve animals out of ivory and

use them as fetishes to help in hunting. They believe that these tiny figures know where land and sea animals are located and can help hunters find them. The Eskimo also carve toys. They make beautiful tops of all shapes and sizes. Some tops are of wood; some are of bone, stone, or even clay. Eskimo children spin the tops on a hard piece of walrus hide, and they while away long hours indoors playing with them. Outdoors

the tops are even more fun, because then the children run around, racing with them. These are not just boys' toys, however. Men like to play with the tops too.

The early traders were much impressed with these carvings and begged the Eskimo to trade them. But the Eskimo refused to sell any of the carvings used as fetishes. The traders also had a hard time trying to get the ivory toys. The toys were owned not by the parents, who carved them, but by the children to whom they were given. And the children refused to part with the toys their fathers or grandfathers had carved for them. Finally, the Eskimo began to carve ivory especially for the traders. These commercial carvings were just as artistic and as carefully done as the fetishes, but the carver did not attach any sacred value to them and so did not mind selling them.

In winter and in summer, the Eskimo greatly enjoy playing games. Because of the restricted space inside the igloo, most indoor games are of a stationary type. One of the oldest and most widespread games in the world is cat's cradle, a game that every Eskimo knows. Cat's cradle is played with a long cord made of twisted sinew. A person twists the cord around the fingers of both hands and makes a pattern that represents an igloo, a lake, a caribou, or a mountain sheep. Another player picks up the cord from the first person's fingers and makes another figure. Figure follows figure, while the players and the audience watch eagerly to see what will come next. An older person may know a complicated figure and save it for last, when the audience is at its largest. Cat's cradle is played in igloos night after night. For the Eskimo it is an especially good game, since it can be played by people sitting close together in a crowded room.

Another favorite is the game of bones—a gambling game. The rules and the manner of playing it vary from one Eskimo group to the next. A circle of men start the game right after the evening meal and keep at it hour after hour,

till everyone is too sleepy to continue. Women play too. The Eskimo use sets of bones that have been specially carved from seal flippers. Each bone has the shape of a certain animal or person. Two players divide the set of bones equally and spread a fur mat between them. Each player picks out a bone, holds it a few inches above the mat, then lets it drop. The bone that lands right side up is the winner. The defeated bone is then

laid aside. The players continue. The man with the victorious bone drops that bone again; the other player drops another bone he has picked from his pile. Again the defeated bone is laid aside. The game is over when one man is completely cleaned out.

Another way to play this game is to throw several of these carved bone animals into the air. When they land, the player who has the most figures standing up and facing him is the winner.

In the summer the Eskimo gather after a day's hunt to wrestle, race, jump rope, and, when the ground permits, play ball. They use a small, light ball, stuffed with hair. The game is played with two goals and two teams. Each team stands near its goal, facing the center. The ball is tossed into the center, and everyone races for it. The object of the game is to throw the ball across the opponent's goal line.

In some parts of the arctic each team forms a line midway between the center and its goal. When the ball is thrown, each side tries to kick it through the line-up and reach their opponents' goal. In other parts of the arctic a free-for-all ball game is played by young and old. The ball is small and light. A stick with a net on the end of it is used to catch the ball and to throw it. Some men can throw a ball a hundred yards.

Women play a sort of hand football. They use a large ball of buckskin, stuffed with hair. A woman strikes the ball with her hand first, then kicks it with her foot. Often young girls team up against married women. They race across the field while the male audience sits on the side lines and encourages them. There is much laughter and teasing from the audience, although everyone admits that the Eskimo girls and women compare well in strength and swiftness with the men and boys.

Another favorite Eskimo game is the toss game. Using a circular piece of walrus skin, a group of Eskimo toss the player into the air by snapping the skin taut. The best players can bounce very high over and over again, never losing their balance and always landing on their feet.

In every settlement there is an old man or woman who excels in storytelling. These people are in great demand. While the stories are being told, the children cuddle up to their parents. Along with their elders, the children seem to enjoy any kind of story, although we might find many of them either very sad or somewhat dull. On the whole, the stories are about supernaturals and about how the world was created. In telling stories about human beings, the storyteller speaks of man's courage, of how he overcomes storms and bests the supernaturals. These are happy tales. But oftentimes, as is true of Eskimo life, the surroundings are too harsh to be overcome by man, and the hero is defeated and dies. Sometimes a story teaches the importance of certain virtues, as in this favorite Eskimo story.

A young, handsome Eskimo did not want to get married. He was lazy and did not care to go hunting all the time to provide for a wife and children. His uncle was a famous shaman and was able, with his knowledge of magic, to get all the seals and caribou they needed. Suddenly the shaman died. All his belongings—his harpoons, his clothing, and his dishes—were buried with him, as is the custom; and there were no more seals and caribou for the young man. Now that he was alone and poor, he hurried to find a rich wife. But the people in the village knew he was lazy

and refused to let him have their daughters. The poor young man remained alone in his cold, bare igloo.

The soul of the departed shaman felt sorry for his nephew, so he built a swift kayak and sped to earth to help him. During the night, while the village slept, the shaman sang his magic songs, invoking the aid of his servant spirits. The young man's igloo turned into a comfortable, fur-lined, spacious home. His tattered clothing became rich skins, trimmed with wolverine fur. A log on the beach became a swift kayak.

The next morning the young man dressed in his beautiful costume and loaded his kayak with furs and sealskins. He paddled across the water to a neighboring village, where he completely overwhelmed the parents of a young girl. They were sure that such a wealthy young man must be a brave and able hunter, and they readily gave him their daughter in marriage.

The happy couple were returning to the young man's igloo when the kayak paddle suddenly cried out, "This is not a kayak. This is a log." The outcry broke the shaman's magic. The young man's clothing turned into tatters again, and his igloo became a miserable, drafty pile of old snow blocks. The bride cried out that she was ill and begged to be taken home.

The young man took her home. Back with his bride's parents he begged his father-in-law to teach him how to use the harpoon and to take him on hunts so he could learn to kill game and support his wife. In time he killed his first seal and gave it to his parents-in-law. The people of the village began to respect the young man. They helped him build an igloo and invited him on hunts, so he could kill enough game for his wife and in-laws.

Marriage customs among the Eskimo differ little from those described in this story. A young man has to ask a girl's parents for her in marriage. Sometimes the young man's parents speak to the girl's parents on his behalf. If the boy is a good hunter, the girl's parents readily agree to the marriage. Otherwise they do not. The young man's parents, of course, know that the girl is a good seamstress and believe she will make him a good wife. Otherwise, they would not have permitted their son to ask for her hand. Sometimes a young man brings gifts to the girl's parents; sometimes he brings a beautiful fur costume for the bride.

There is no marriage ceremony. Having received her parents' consent, the girl follows the young man to his home, unless her parents ask him to stay with them. If the young man's home is too crowded, the couple will build one for themselves. The young wife brings with her only her sewing kit and a bundle of sinew. It is up to her husband to provide everything from now on.

An Eskimo wife is expected to let her husband do all the talking when other men, especially strangers, are present. It is considered poor manners for a woman to speak up in public, and it would embarrass everyone. At home, however, husband and wife talk things over, and often he is guided by her advice. When a hunter brings home game, it is up to the housewife to apportion the food and decide what will be stored for the future. She also decides when she will tan the skins and how they will be used.

Among themselves the women are very talkative. Nothing escapes them. Since they travel less than the men do and are cut off from the outside world, they are all ears whenever the men gather to talk. When a woman learns something new, she tells her friends about it the moment they get together. Since the Eskimo live in very small settlements, nothing ever happens in one household that the rest of the neighbors do not know about. But although there is much gossip, people have great respect for each other's feelings. They never criticize anyone directly, for this would be too embarrassing and might cause a family to leave the settlement. Instead, if a person has been stingy about sharing his catch with his neighbors, no one accuses him or his wife directly. But the next time the hunter's wife brings a neighbor a very small piece of meat and blubber, the neighbor's wife will present the stingy woman with a pile of skins. The skins, of course, are worth a hundred times more than the meat. The stingy Eskimo realizes what the neighbors think of her and her husband. Thoroughly ashamed, she rushes home and returns with her husband and children, laden with meat and blubber. Husband and wife pile the food on top of the skins and beg the offended neighbor to take back the skins and accept the food.

At certain times of the year, when they have accumulated enough furs and when their supplies of ammunition, coffee, tea, and sugar have been exhausted, Eskimo families go to the trading post. When the husband and his wife enter the trading post, they set down their bags of fox pelts and bearskins in an inconspicuous place. They do not want the trader to feel that they are there on business, for this would not be polite. In turn, they would be offended if the trader asked them outright what they had to trade. Instead, the

Eskimo and the trader treat each other as old friends. The trader serves them coffee and inquires about their health, their children, their neighbors, their dogs, what games they have been playing, and what kind of weather they have had. In reply to the couple's questions, the trader tells them all the news of the post and perhaps something about the outside world.

The couple may camp near the trading post for a few days, joining in the social life that goes on around there—evening gatherings, games, wrestling matches, and feasting. At last they decide that it is time to return home. They go to the trading post early in the morning. Again they are served coffee, and the trader finally asks them what is in the bags they have brought with them. This brings forth a loud laugh from the hunter, seconded by his wife. "One is carrying some old things in those bags," the Eskimo says. "There is nothing in them worth showing to a friend who has such fine things in his store. One happens to be a very poor hunter who does not have the skill to get a good fox pelt." The hunter's wife beams at this speech. Her husband talks so well.

The trader persists in wanting to see what is inside the bags, and the hunter continues his apologies. The other Eskimo in the store are filled with curiosity and crowd around the counter. Finally the woman brings over the bags and slowly, reluctantly, as though blushing with shame for her poor husband, opens one of them and takes out a few fox pelts. Eagerly, the husband and wife watch the expressions on the faces of their audience, especially the trader's expression. They grin at the oh's and ah's of admiration. The trader exclaims, "Never before have I seen such beautiful pelts!" And he is telling the truth. The pelts are, indeed, beautiful and lustrous. The Eskimo couple, of course, know they are, for the woman has carefully tanned and brushed the pelts and has spent weeks scraping the fat off them.

It is now the trader's turn to be modest. He says that he does not have anything in his stock worthy of such fine pelts. With many apologies, he leads the couple into his storeroom to select the things they want. It is not unusual for all the Eskimo customers at the trading post to accompany the couple into the storeroom and help them make their selections. Everyone knows, of course, that the couple have given the matter much thought. They have talked over every detail during the winter evenings, while working on the pelts. The man knows exactly what ammunition he will need; the woman knows she needs needles and groceries and things for the children.

Having had the fun of handling every item in the trader's stock, the couple make their selections. They protest that they are getting too much for their poor pelts, and the trader begs them to accept the goods he is stuffing into their bags. In the end, the couple depart with a fully loaded sled, satisfied with the trading.

As already mentioned, some Eskimo believe that Anguta and Sedna created the earth and everything on it; others believe that Raven was the creator. In addition, the Eskimo say, there are many spirits, some stronger than others. In fact, everything in the Eskimo's world has a spirit: rocks, trees, bushes, winds, clouds, animals, fishes, and icebergs. Each of these also has a shade spirit, which has the power to roam about at will. The Eskimo often invite the shades to attend ceremonials and festivals, for they believe this will ensure success in hunting.

A man or woman who has strange dreams decides that the supernaturals want him or her to become a shaman. This man or woman becomes apprenticed to an older shaman and learns his craft and tricks, such as ventriloquism and the curing of illnesses. Some Eskimo shamans claim that they can change the weather, predict future events, and even go up to the moon. The Eskimo believe that the great manlike being in the moon controls all the game on earth. When there is starvation among the Eskimo, a shaman often volunteers to take a trip to the moon to plead with the moon being to release the animals to the hunters. The shaman vanishes for a while from his home. When he returns, he has a message from the moon being. It may be that game will come soon; it may be directions telling the hunters where game can be found.

All Eskimo wear amulets to protect themselves against evil and witchcraft. These amulets may be feathers, animal teeth, or just a piece of rock. Since a child's first fur suit is considered to have sacred powers, an adult sometimes wears a piece of it as his amulet. Amulets are put into tiny leather bags that are worn around the neck. When an Eskimo dies, his amulet is buried with him. It will protect him and guide him on his journey to the other worlds.

The Eskimo have a serene attitude toward death. When a person dies, they say that the spirits have willed it. Every time a hunter leaves his igloo, he is never sure whether or not he will return. Sudden storms, so common in the arctic, may spring up, and the best hunter can lose his way and starve to death or drown. When this happens, the family mourns its loss for a while, then returns to the daily problems of providing food. During these days of mourning, a successful hunter will go to the bereaved household and leave generous slices of blubber and meat. He does this quietly, almost apologetically, so the widow will not feel obligated. "Here is a little piece of something," he says humbly. "Even your dogs won't eat it."

The Eskimo never speak of their dead by name, but they are anxious that the dead person should have a namesake just as soon as possible. The first baby born after a person's death inherits that name, so a boy may inherit the name of a woman. It is believed that the spirit of the dead person enters the baby's body and gives it additional strength and power.

Offerings to honor the dead are made by their relatives throughout the year. Clothing and small bowls of food and water are left outdoors, where the shades of the dead are likely to wander. The purpose of these offerings is to keep the shades warm and fed. The Eskimo believe that each person has two or three shades or souls. One remains with the body; the other two wander about for a while near the dead person's home. Eventually the shades go up to the sky or underground. The relatives do not worry over those who have died violent deaths, for they soon go up to the sky, where there is ample food and water. However, the shades of people who have died normal deaths go underground, where there is no food or water. These shades must be fed for some time, so the relatives continue making the offerings.

In addition to these offerings, the nearest relative begins to save skins, furs, carvings, and tobacco. In a few years he joins with other people in the village in a great feast to celebrate the dead. This feast lasts several days, and during it the hosts give away all the goods they have accumulated. Now the shades of their dead relatives underground are satisfied.

The Eskimo also have ceremonies and feasts to honor the animals, so the hunters will have ample game in the coming year. In Alaska the first annual ceremony of this kind is the inviting-in feast. Long before it is held, hunters begin to carve wooden masks to represent heads of animals. Some shamans carve the heads of supernaturals; others carve the heads of beings from Eskimo stories. The masks are all sizes and shapes. Some are so large that they cannot be carried and are hung from the ceiling of the ceremonial house. Their owners stand under them during the ceremonial, dancing and chanting.

Shades of all the animals represented by the masks are called upon to come and enjoy the singing and dancing in their honor. Food and water are offered to them. When the ceremony is finished, the masks are usually burned. If a man wants to keep his mask, he must substitute a similar piece of wood and put it in the fire.

The bladder festival is another winter ceremonial in honor of the game, and it lasts several days. Everyone takes part in it, and there is dancing, singing, and feasting. Hunters bring in the bladders of the seals, walruses, whales, and bears they have caught, and tie them up on their harpoons. Each day these bladders are painted and decorated. On the last day of the ceremonial, the bladders are carried out and sunk through a hole in the ice.

All important ceremonies take place in winter, when the villages are full, and they usually last for several days. A few neighboring villages may get together for an important celebration. Due to the influence of missionaries among all Eskimo groups, many of these ceremonies have been changed, and some have been abandoned altogether. Other ceremonies are practiced secretly, to avoid outside interference.

By attending these ceremonies and watching their elders, Eskimo children learn about religion. And by watching their elders in other activities—hunting and fishing, building igloos, working and playing at home, trading at the trading post—they acquire the skills and attitudes necessary for survival in the arctic regions.

7

EXPLORING THE ARCTIC

In the early days many European explorers—
the Norsemen, the British, the Dutch, and the
Russians—braved the merciless ice and cold, the
sudden violent winds and storms, the floating
pack ice, and the hot and muddy summers of the
unknown arctic. All of them sought a shorter
passage to the fabulously rich lands of India and
China, then known as Cathay. Although these
early explorers used the stars to locate points on
the earth, mapping was very inaccurate. Many
an explorer went astray, and many made mistakes
that cost them their lives. In order to successfully
explore and map the arctic, these men had to
adopt Eskimo ways and receive Eskimo help and
guidance. Today the arctic is still being explored,

and the Eskimo, as ever, serve as guides and helpers.

It is believed that in 330 B.C. a Greek philos-
opher and mathematician by the name of Pytheas
of Marseille sailed from Scotland to Iceland and
continued about a hundred miles beyond. Perhaps
he might have been the first explorer to reach
Greenland, the stepping stone to the arctic, but
the ice packs made him turn back.

Twelve centuries after Pytheas, the first successful voyage from Iceland to Greenland was
made by Eric the Red. Eric was a Norwegian
chieftain and a sea rover, who had been living in
Iceland. Never a man who got along peacefully
with his neighbors, he started a feud with the Ice-
landic colonists and was declared an outlaw.
About 980 he and his followers sailed west across
the Strait of Denmark for the unknown and spent
the next three years exploring the southern and
western coasts of Greenland. Eric then sailed
back to Iceland to get colonists. He left Iceland
with twenty-five ships, but only fourteen of them

reached the protected western coast of Greenland.
There he founded two colonies: one at what is
now Julianehaab, the other at Godthaab.

Greenland was already inhabited. The Norsemen made friends with the fur-clad, cheerful
men, women, and children. The new settlers were
anxious to learn the ways of the Eskimo hunter.
They exchanged gifts and traded for meat and
blubber.

With the help of their new friends, Eric, and

later his son, Leif Ericson, continued to explore the western coast of Greenland. They also may have sailed into what were later named Davis Strait and Baffin Bay, although this is not certain. They, like later explorers, soon found out that the Eskimo knew their geography well.

The British explorers who followed the Norsemen were not interested in settling in the arctic. They were seeking a northwest passage that would take them to the riches of the East. As yet, no one suspected the existence of the Pacific Ocean. John Cabot, a Venetian in the service of the English, and his son, Sebastian, explored and mapped Labrador and what was later named Baffin Island.

In 1576 another British explorer, Sir Martin Frobisher, wandered in and out of Davis Strait and what were later to be named Frobisher Bay and Cumberland Sound. But Frobisher did not know where he was. In Frobisher Bay he encountered Eskimo for the first time. After seeing their yellowish complexion, narrow eyes, and high cheekbones, he concluded that they were Chinese and thought that he had at last reached Cathay. For a while Frobisher's trip was considered a great success, since he returned to England with soil which was thought to contain gold. The Cathay Gold Mining Company was organized, and an expedition was outfitted to go and mine more of the precious ore. Later, experts looked at the soil more carefully and discovered that the yellow coloring was not gold. The company folded up and declared itself bankrupt.

In 1577 and 1578 Frobisher went on two more expeditions. On one of them he missed Frobisher Bay entirely and instead entered for a short distance what was to be named Hudson Strait. Later he did explore Frobisher Bay and found that it had no western outlet.

The next important arctic explorer was John Davis, who sailed from England in 1585 and landed near Godthaab in Greenland. He then sailed westward into Davis Strait. In the diaries Davis kept he noted that he met Eskimo near the

Godthaab harbor. The Eskimo greeted him with welcoming shouts but did not rush aboard as they had in the past. By this time they had become more wary of these ships and wanted to make sure that the strangers would not mistreat them as others had done. The crew danced and sang to attract the Eskimo. After a while one of the Eskimo pointed to the sun and then struck his chest. He was asking the crew to promise not to mistreat him. A sailor, imitating the Eskimo's gesture, also pointed to the sun and struck his chest. This seemed to satisfy the Eskimo. He and several other men climbed aboard. There they shook hands with everyone and, Davis further recorded, kissed his hand. Since handshaking and kissing are not Eskimo customs, it is obvious that these Eskimo had had some contact with Europeans who had shown them these new customs.

Davis was impressed with the seaworthiness and lightness of the Eskimo kayaks and asked the Eskimo to trade with him. The Eskimo readily exchanged kayaks, clothing, and food for metal knives, hatchets, files, and guns. Then the crew cleared a space on deck for wrestling matches with the Eskimo. They were surprised at the Eskimo's skill, strength, and nimbleness, despite their thick-set appearance.

At first Davis was impressed with the Eskimo's friendliness, simplicity, and eagerness to help him. But when he went on an exploring trip and returned some days later, he found that they had taken some of his iron, paddles, and cloth. He and his crew regarded this as stealing, unaware that Eskimo customs permit a man to use a friend's things if he needs them. This misunderstanding led to Davis's change of attitude toward the Eskimo. The Eskimo, on the other hand, remained as friendly as ever, though puzzled that they were no longer invited aboard.

On one of his exploring trips Davis turned westward and entered Cumberland Sound in Baffin Island. But he had no idea that he was in new waters. The wind changed and Davis, expecting a fierce arctic storm, hurried back. On another exploring trip he sailed north along Davis Strait to Baffin Bay. He was stopped by ice packs and turned back. On the way back he skirted along the coast of Baffin Island and turned into Hudson Strait. He is credited with discovering Cape Chidley, the northeastern tip of Labrador.

In 1609 Henry Hudson, an Englishman who served the Muscovy Company of London merchants, discovered the Hudson River. While studying the ice formations between Spitsbergen and Greenland, he found the island of Jan Mayen. In 1610 Hudson also discovered and named Hudson Bay, which he entered through Hudson Strait.

In 1615 and 1616 William Baffin searched for a northwest passage. He sailed around and mapped Baffin Bay and the northwest coast of Baffin Island. Baffin is also credited with mapping Lancaster Sound, Jones Sound, and Smith Sound.

When the Hudson's Bay Company incorporated in 1670, the English were no longer interested in finding a route to the rich Indies, for they were finding riches right there in the arctic. Hudson's Bay employees traveled by land and sea, exploring rivers, bays, and islands. They began mapping the Arctic Archipelago and establishing fur-trading centers.

Sir Alexander Mackenzie, an employee of another trading company, the North Western Company, traveled northward from Great Slave Lake and followed the then unknown Mackenzie River to its mouth, where it empties into Mackenzie Bay. Mackenzie also went up the Peace River and found and named the Fraser River. Through one of its tributaries he reached the Pacific coast. Mackenzie, therefore, made the first overland journey north of Mexico to the Pacific. Balboa, of course, had discovered the Pacific Ocean over a century earlier, in 1513.

It was up to Vitus Bering, a Dane in the service of Russia's tsar, Peter the Great, and his successor, Catherine I, to prove that North America and Asia were separated. In 1728 Vitus Bering sailed into Bering Strait and gave it its name. Russia quickly sent settlers to the New World to lay claim to the northwest coast of North America. Russian explorers and traders eventually penetrated as far south as California and ended up by claiming Alaska and the Aleutian Islands. These possessions were purchased from Russia by William Henry Seward in 1867 for $7,200,000, giving the United States a handsome foothold in the Arctic zone—a territory of almost 600,000 square miles.

The studying, mapping, and exploring of the arctic went on, interrupted only by European wars, when government and private funds became tied up elsewhere. By the middle of the nineteenth century the arctic regions had been well mapped. When Sir John Franklin's expedition of 1845-48 was lost, some forty expeditions from various nations went out, in the course of the next twenty years, to search for it. The Eskimo, with their knowledge of the region, served as guides for these expeditions and supplied sleds, dogs, and food. Among those who set out to find the lost

Franklin expedition were several American explorers. One of them, Charles Hall, succeeded in tracing Franklin's route, but no members of the Franklin expedition were ever found. The agony of their last days is still hidden in the arctic.

By the end of the nineteenth century several nations decided to co-operate in studying the Arctic Circle. These nations established stations in the arctic and sent groups of scientists there to gather information about meteorological and atmospheric conditions and about arctic plants and animals.

In the beginning of the twentieth century, two major challenges remained. One was to travel from the Atlantic to the Pacific entirely by boat through a northwest passage. This was accomplished by Roald Amundsen, a Norwegian, between 1903 and 1905. Amundsen started out from Norway. He crossed the Atlantic and proceeded through the straits and bays of the Arctic Archipelago to the Bering Sea and thence to the Pacific Ocean.

The other challenge was to reach the North Pole. It was due to the persistence of Robert Edwin Peary of the United States Navy that the first flag to fly over the North Pole was that of the United States. Between 1891 and 1905 Peary made several expeditions to the arctic to study the land and its people, and in 1905 he came within 200 miles of the North Pole. He had to turn back, however, for his ships could not pass through the ice around the Pole.

Peary put the entire expedition on sleds, and he and his men advanced in small groups. One group blazed a trail for the sleds, to avoid wearing out the dogs. They also built igloos, so that those in the rear, who carried most of the supplies and were, therefore, more tired at the end of a day's march, could find ready shelters. It is interesting to note that of the 650-pound load each sled carried, 500 pounds consisted of food for the dogs.

Pushing on and on, Peary finally reached 89.57 degrees north latitude on April 6, 1909. There he buried a glass bottle with a strip of his flag inside it and formally took possession of the North Pole in the name of the President of the United States. As Peary later wrote, it was only with the help of the Eskimo and their dogs that he was able to reach the North Pole. Without them he could not have done it.

Between 1926 and 1928 the first polar flights were made—something the old explorers had dreamed of for many years. Commander Richard Byrd of the United States Navy flew from Spitsbergen to the North Pole and back in only sixteen hours. Two days later Roald Amundsen, with Lincoln Ellsworth and Umberto Nobile, an Italian, crossed the North Pole and reached Teller, Alaska, in seventy-one hours. Later, in May of 1928, General Nobile made another flight but was wrecked on the ice east of Spitsbergen. Nobile and most of his crew were saved. Amundsen, however, who rushed to help find them, perished.

Although the arctic has attracted explorers for over 2000 years, there is still much in this region that is unexplored and unknown. Only two years

ago, in August of 1957, a mountain a mile in
height was found in the Arctic Ocean, near the
North Pole. This discovery was made by several
scientists, who camped on the ice floes to do re-

search during the International Geophysical Year.
They measured the depth of the water where this
mountain protruded and found it to be 5000 feet
high. Its width and length are still to be determined. Also, there is much talk that Greenland,

as we know it today, is two islands instead of one. The theory is that the icecap of Greenland binds the land together. This needs further exploring. Perhaps one day in the process of studying the icecap, explorers will also find out more about the land underneath.

Today the arctic regions are very important as airplane bases and as sources of weather information. They will become even more important in the future as missile bases. The scientists who go there now still look to the Eskimo for friendly help and hospitality.

INDEX

* Indicates illustrations

157